D0449029

Near the Mountains

Joseph Bruchac

WHITE PINE PRESS

Copyright 1987 by Joseph Bruchac

ACKNOWLEDGEMENTS

I would like to express my thanks to the following publications where some of these poems first appeared: *Arachne, Alembic, The Ark, Cedar Rock, Blueline, The Ark, The Chariton Review, Common Sense, The Connecticut Poetry Review, Footprint, Granite, The Hampden-Sydney Poetry Review, The Hawaii Review, The Hudson Review, Light, The Nation, New Letters, Memphis State Review, The Mid-American Review, Mudfish, Northwest Review, The Ohio Review, Organic Gardening, Paintbrush, The Paris Review, Poetry Australia, Poetry Now, Porch, Prism International, Quaterly West, Raccoon, Shantih, Sing Heavenly Muse, The Small Farm, Stand, The Syracuse Scholar, Tendril, Washout Review,* and *Whetstone.*

Some of these poems appeared in the following out of print chapbooks:

FLOW, Cold Mountain Press, Austin, Texas, 1975.
THIS EARTH IS A DRUM, Cold Mountain Press, Austin,Texas, 1976.
ANCESTRY, Great Raven Press, Fort Kent, Maine, 1980.
ENTERING ONONDAGA, Cold Mountain Press, Austin, Texas, 1978.

I would also like to express my thanks to the New York State Creative Artists Program and to the National Endowmant for the Arts for Poetry Fellowships which helped make possible the writing of many of these poems.

This publication was made possible, in part, by grants from the New York State Council on the Arts and the National Endowment for the Arts.

Design by Watershed Design

Cover illustration by Rokwaho. Reprinted with permission from *Covers,* published by Strawberry Press.

WHITE PINE PRESS
76 Center Street
Fredonia, New York 14063

CONTENTS

Part Three: Near The Mountains

This book is dedicated to my wife and best friend, Carol, and to the memory of two friends and teachers whose words and spirits remain with me: Lawrence Older and Swift Eagle.

THE BALANCE

ONE HOT SUMMER NIGHT, 1947

One hot summer night,
Old Mr. Luther
breast-stroked up the hill
from the Cascades Bar and Grill.

His eyes were glassy
as creekbed stones.
He thought he was on
the Milky Way, floating
into the Big Dipper.

My grandfather stayed
in his chair near the pumps,
under the lights
where big moths whirred
drunken in the glare.

My grandmother loaded
the old man into her car.
I climbed, unnoticed,
into the back.

Floating, his head
half out the window,
Mr. Luther mumbled
a little song to the treetops
all the way to Corinth
while my grandmother sat
Samaritan stern,
stiff as Church
behind the wheel,
moving against the tide
and never confusing
the road with the stars.

SLOPPING THE HOGS, 1951

My grandfather handed me the bucket,
day just breaking down Splinterville Hill.
Then, eyes still filled with sleep,
leaned to one side against the weight,
I trudged out to the Little House lean-to
where the smell of pigs was strong
as the scent of ferment from the galvanized pail.

"Sooooo-eeeee, pigpigpig," I called,
voice thin in the throat of dawn.
My stick cracked ice in their trough
as hogs stirred up from straw,
mud tinkling like bells under trotters,
frost in the weeds a froth of diamond.

One leg over the fence as they rooted,
bristled backs rough against my wrist
I leaned out to touch once, quick,
a nose aglisten like a doll's china face,
thinking of pig lore I'd been taught,
how a boar would eat anything—even a snake.

I'd heard of the boy up North Creek Road
who fell into the pen and was eaten by pigs
his farmer father still slaughtered for bacon,
yet I swayed back and forth, innocent in my balance.

Slops for the hogs—say it with me now, friends,
as I call, call myself with simple words
which ease back that fence-sitting dawn,
defying even the dreams of falling.

BIRDFOOT'S GRAMPA

The old man
must have stopped our car
two dozen times to climb out
and gather into his hands
the small toads blinded
by our lights and leaping,
live drops of rain.

The rain was falling,
a mist about his white hair
and I kept saying
you can't save them all
accept it, get back in
we've got places to go.

But, leathery hands full
of wet brown life
knee deep in the summer
roadside grass,
he just smiled and said
they have places to go
too

3

PHOTO OF THE OLD HOUSE

for Donald Hall

I know the house
though I have never
been through its doors
or scuffed the leaves
of maple trees
which shade the roof
from sun and storm.
Stones handled by
the wash of a creek
grow smooth, familiar
to the touch.
So, too, the lives
of those who follow
the path worn by
an ancestor's feet.

You returned to the land,
soil made familiar
by the plod of horses,
sweat, blood and spit.

You returned to words
which, like old wood,
split-ash shingles and
hand-hewn chestnut beams,
keep the scent of
a hundred springs.

One hand on the lintel,
you lean into the stance
of your grandfather's voice.
There, where nothing ended,
you begin again.

RELICS

The arrowheads my grandfather found
his eyes always quick for the flash of flint
rest in a dusty White Owls box in the attic.

It is only in the golden Corn, the twining Beans
and the bright skins of Squash
that I can begin to touch the hands
of the Longhouse People who kept this land.

THE BALANCE

He found the stone ax in his field,
plowing one spring to put in corn.
I remember him holding it on his palm,
weathered as that flint chipped by one
whose voice would always be silent to me
as the story he told, weighing it the way
another might heft a gold piece, then
placing it carefully in my hands.

5

TWO PICTURES OF MY SLOVAK GRANDPARENTS, 1914

I.

Her feet stitch the sidewalks
of the Garment District.
It is gray in those stories
as the woolen shawls
of Middle European women.

Her fingers are thin,
polished bone spools.

II.

The sun peers down on him
through coal smoke clouds.
It squints like the Asian eye
of a Slovak steelworker.

His breath is hesitant
from seared lungs,
whitens the throat
of the winter sky.

III.

My uncles may not recognize
their parents in these words.
The images are strange to them
as that language they learned
is to me—a tongue
which never gathered money,
although it warmed them
as they shared it, one fire
they could always afford.

DEAD SKIN

The porcelain basin filled with water,
the black chair in the middle of the kitchen,
and on the table my grandfather's jackknife—
to cut away dead skin from her soles.

I see my grandmother bending there,
her heavy arms reaching down
to lift her feet, small as a girl's,
from water smoky with drifting soap.

The knife was sharp and tissue fell
like apple parings or potato peels,
leaving behind the clean pink flesh
she wanted to see, Methodist pure.

Sometimes she slipped, then water caught
small drops of red and her poor feet
hurt too much for her to continue.
Then she would give the chair to me.

But I could never learn her knack
for cutting just enough of the callous
without going too deeply in and
even the skin which was horny and dead
I sneaked into my mouth and ate—
keeping those impure parts of myself
which nothing she did ever rid me of,
not her anger or her sorrow.

MORNING SONG

My grandfather always rose with the sun.
It was his oldest friend.

The front door of the general store he ran
faced toward the east and he'd sit there
in a blue painted chair of pine cut from his woods,
waiting for those first rays to touch his face.

He grew stronger as the light moved higher,
hands moving like crickets coming back to life
among grass blades frosted overnight.

Then, before he'd stand to his long day's work,
he'd lift his palms and hold them there,
just long enough to cup the sun.

GASHER BROOK

After three decades
of drawing water
and not long after
the departure
of the last of ten
whose birthings left
her body loose
as a freshet's flow,
she walked away
from the evening house,
her husband's heavy snore.

At its deepest,
where they dipped the bucket,
no more than up
to a horse's knees
she wedged her head
beneath a stone.

I guess that was
the only way
she ever did know
any sort of peace,
her brother said to me,
ten miles further
on down the road,
more years after
her life
than she lived.

CATTAIL WIND

Go to the meadow behind Braim's pond
when the day moves slow into night

Let the laughter of those
who live by comparisons
lift from you like the mist
now rising from the alders

The cattail wind feathers the evening
shadows coalesce in the sky
beyond Orion's slanted belt
cold fireflies of time
old messages for your eyes

If you wait long enough
two things will come

the deer, eyes glowing
with the valleys of the moon

the dawn, uneven as
the edge of wind-brushed feathers

They will touch your face
leave you
changed

This is no warning
it is a map

CUTTING THE POTATOES

It was a ritual of late April—
knives honed on
the foot-pedal grindstone,
seed stock brought
from the dark root cellar.

Then my grandmother, grandfather and I
would cut the potatoes into sections,
each piece holding that small green knob
which I had learned to call an eye—
a heartbeat waiting to pump life in
from soil and rain to form other selves
round as the cycle of seasons.

The skins were leather,
the flesh beneath firm.
Small beads of moisture sprang
before the pressure of the blade.
Cut just enough to feed the shoots,
enough to make the harvest full.

We'd leave them then
in the air to harden
overnight making a blue skin
against worms and the threat of rot.
Next day, two feet apart,
we'd plant them in rows,
each with a handful of manure
beneath the warm blanket of earth.

What did I learn
those early springs—
that a blade should be sharp
to cut edges clean?
To measure the difference
between excess and loss?
To have patience till time,
like the soil, was right?

Or just to trust
in that slow orbit of roots
where what we save may multiply,
return another year.

ALFALFA

Burlap bag held firm,
stretched between your heels,
you bend, grab loose handfuls, then
stuff them back between your legs
like a dog digging for a bone.

Alfalfa smell
fills sinuses, dust
from dry stems
drifts into hair.
Small insects flutter
up from stubble.
Past the distant edge
of the field, a brown thrasher
sings in locust trees—
a voice cool as water.

As you shuffle forward,
bags fill up fast,
musty logs hefted
up into the truck
where, hours later,
you lie at last,
hands green as the grass
which clings to wet skin,
riding five hundred
bags of alfalfa, mouth
open to drink the wind.

DUNHAM BROOK

All the streams
in Greenfield Center
were running slow
from the drought of late summer
when I went with dusk
to Dunham Brook.

Wood ducks,
their crests bright rainbows,
spoke to each other
from both sides of the swamp.
A bittern boomed
the coming dark.
Bullfrogs held
the breath of evening
to let it go
again and again
in deep drumbeats.

Rain dappled the surface
of water flowing,
flowing alive and dark
into the mouth.
I thought for one moment
how I might look—
a moving tree against the sky
seen by a trout.

Then the worm vanished
and the line pulled steady
with a pulse.

THE MAP

When the old man called me over
to his truck by our outside pump,
I knew something was up
by the look in his eye.

"Want me to fill it, Mr. Sokol?" I said,
but he gestured me close enough to see
the snowy forest of hairs on his broad forearm.

"Let's yust see how shtrong you got to be,"
he said, crooking is finger out
like the handle of a coffee cup.

He linked it with mine, then said, "Hokay!"
Now pull me out, Yozef! PULL ME OUT, I SAID!"

And I pulled, feeling bone grind against bone,
knuckles popping like corks as he braced himself,
left hand holding the wheel as I pulled back, pulled
until he reached the edge of his seat—
then I loosened up, let him pull me in.

"Good boy, Yozef! Good boy!" he said,
his left hand exploding into my shoulder.
"Good boy! Anno! You gettin' shtrong!"

I nodded and smiled, still seeing the pattern
of blue veins formed on his straining forehead—
a map of the Old Country, its strength
and pain linked into my blood.

PLUMS

Grandma Bruchac lies with closed eyes,
her hair blue as the skin of a plum,
that color because she washed it before
beginning dinner—the pots were bubbling
on the iron stove when she had the stroke.

In the neatly-made hospital bed
she has slept three days, a traveller
gaining strength before climbing one final hill.
The blue of European plums surrounds
her face like flower petals
or fingers stained from picking fruit.

Her face, a pale cloud, drifts further away.
She dreams of Turnava, where the boy
she'll marry years later in this land is waiting.
He has brought her something from his uncle's orchard.
Her hand moves from yours to accept that gift.

15

OLD TOOLS

OLD TOOLS

Heaped in boxes
in cluttered back buildings,
returning to the red of ore
among patented planters
and bits of horse harness,
I find reminders
of the soil which shaped
the bones of my lineage.

Broad-bitted ax, spokeshave,
and rat-tailed rasp—
familiar to me as names,
not from callouses formed.
Yet, cleaned, honed
back to brightness,
this well-used steel
can do its work.

In these tools I feel
my great-grandfather's hands,
begin to read the lines of his life
in my own palms
and the mysteries
of an old tough way
which, like a new-cut ashwood handle
fitted into a splitting maul,
my life begins to enter.

PRAYER

Let my words
be bright with animals,
images the flash of a gull's wing.
If we pretend
that we are at the center,
that moles and kingfishers,
eels and coyotes
are at the edge of grace,
then we circle, dead moons
about a cold sun.
This morning I ask only
the blessing of the crayfish,
the beatitude of the birds;
to wear the skin of the bear
in my songs;
to work like a man with my hands.

GOING THROUGH SEED CATALOGUES IN LATE WINTER

Some people say nothing can ever taste
as good as it looks on those glossy pages
where corn is creamy as August clouds
and the red of tomatoes is rich as blood.

You'll sow only for weeds and the woodchucks,
they say, but as I write down the names of plants:
Red Chantenay, Trophy and Scarlet Nantes,
Gemini, Sweet Slice and China Cucumber,
Stuttgarter Onion sets, Summer Festival melon,
I know these words are an incantation.

As I speak them snow leaves our fence rows
and the wings of birds begin to answer,
coming up the long flyways home.

FEEDER

Each time I fill
the bird feeder I made
from old cellar wood
nailed to the cut-off
stub of an ancient
lilac tree

I feel the claws
of the chickadees
on my finger, their beaks
prodding the crevices
of my hands which hold
seeds of the sun.

They are perfectly solemn
full of purpose and joy,
and I watch them
from my human distance
which does not always
come between us.

GLUSKABI AND THE MAPLE TREE

Long ago, they say,
the maple tree
gave pure syrup
every spring.

The Indian people
just had to break
a twig and then
lie down beneath
with their mouths open
to catch the sweetness.

Gluskabi saw
his Indian people
were getting lazy.
This will never do.

So he took many buckets
of water from the river
and poured them into
the tops of the trees.

Now my people will have to work.
They'll have to sweat
to get their syrup.
They'll have to make fires,
cut dead wood from the forest
and collect many buckets
for each bucket of syrup.

And so it has been to this day.

DRINKING FROM THE MAPLE BUCKETS

1.

Night cups its hand over the hill.
My feet slip on stones buried by March snow
as I pick my way through saplings
which grasp at my shirt with tiny fingers.

Looking back upslope, lights from windows blind me
until I remember one must shade one's eyes
against human lights to see a path in darkness.

2.

Through the branches,
smooth, cold as onyx,
a firefly glitters—
the Evening Star.

3.

Lifting the first pail,
I sip water which flows
against earth's weight.
A clean light taste
clings to my lips.

Then, glimpsing a pattern
in the bottom of the bucket,
I raise my head, see above me
the Big Dipper pouring
the clear liquid
of this night upon my face.

TWO NIGHTS BEFORE THE FIRST DAY OF SPRING

Stoking the wood stove for the night,
an ember of elm falls onto the tray.
It makes us think of strawberries
glowing from the back field in June.

For three nights now the flying squirrels
which nest in our attic have waked us near dawn,
their thumping the steps of small shy ghosts.

Saying goodnight to our sons,
all of us can taste spring coming.
We're excited, find it hard to sleep.
"Is our house really haunted?" they ask.
I tell them again no monsters hide
in closets or piles of slumped clothes.
What we feel here protects us.

Jesse remembers one night last summer
when he saw in the woods by the field
a pool, a circle of little chairs,
small shapes dancing light in darkness.
"Dad, I felt like I'd been given
something, like it was a gift."

Good night, we say, good night, good night.
Closing our doors only part way,
no walls between our dreams.

FORKING MANURE

Tim Hardhild's fork slides easy in,
lifts away the dark top layer
of straw from the stalls of thirty Guernseys.
Beneath, manure golden as corn
squishes under boots as we bend
to load the pick-up.

His father is in the hospital,
stroke yesterday at fifty-two.
It's three o'clock in the afternoon,
a Saturday, but soon the man
from the U.F.O., his tank truck shiny
as a flying saucer, will come to take
the day's milking for Amsterdam dairies.
"Your day about half over now?" I ask.
He laughs, "Not hardly a quarter."

Just seventeen, he knows how hard
it is to work the land. He's one who didn't go away
to a GE job or another state.
His hands already rough, his voice
like his father's is soft,
spoken half to the earth.

I finish shovelling, watch him even off
our ten-dollar load with a dozen more forks.
If he moves, will there be another?
Who will cut the corn,
turn the rusty bolts,
when the Hardhilds are gone,
leaving fields to brush?

But as I pay him, his eyes are following
the line of cows up a long-grazed hill
and though he hears my words,
I know it's not for me he's smiling.

COMPOST

On a bright day in the Planting Moon
we turn a pile built for two years,
all the scraps from long-eaten meals,
the tops of carrots, radishes, beets,
apple peels and potato skins, bad spots
from apples, strawberries, tomatoes,
and all those things which might have lain
growing foul among cans and cardboard
buried in a landfill.

Instead we saved them, carried them
even through January snows
into the field between house and creek,
mixed in hay, last autumn's leaves,
cow manure and the ashes from a Franklin stove.

The spading fork sinks into the pile
and beneath the surface, dark as coal
among egg shells glittering like ancestors' skulls
we find a lode of rich new earth,
sweet to smell, clinging to hands
like the good duff of forest leaves.

Even my hands feel ready to sprout
strong roots and grow green
as we work this offering
into the soil of the season's first plantings.

FINDING ARROWHEADS

Though I've walked fields
where my grandfather
picked up bird points,
lance tips and hatchet blades,
those bones of earth
have never met my eyes.

But I never followed a plow,
my feet learning
the horse's rhythm,
back leaning into the reins,
blade parting earth
as a ship parts a wave.

And my own springs
are less than half
of those he walked,
the way a deer
walks into a meadow
where snow has melted.

So, each year
in the Planting Moon,
I walk the new soil,
watch my hands lose
the paleness of winter,
and trust that when
the time is right
words of stone will find me.

RADISHES

First seeds in
when the snow still hovers
like a Snowy Owl ready to fly,
pausing before its final departure,
the radishes, round as small pink rocks
roll off my palm and into the row
drawn with an index finger.

Then I cover
my small advance guard
of dragon's tooth soldiers,
knowing they will lift green plumes
before other crops have even left
the brown bags and sealed seed cartons
stacked on a back-room shelf.

First to leave my hands, first to return
one day in late May when I pull red globes,
my teeth feeling the crisp white flesh
within the biting taste of the skin,
this year's renewal of the old pledge,
between my blood and this soil,
a pact which began long before
I saw my grandfather's hand pack down
spring earth brown as his fingers.

TOMATO PLANTS

Small swaying fronds,
Fred Braim pulls them
out of the beds
in his old green house
where a rusted Warm Morning stove
stands inside the door
and windowpanes overhead
cracked by hail three summers ago
are covered with clear plastic.

He dips the plants in a yellow pail,
wraps muddy roots in wet *Saratogians,*
and ties them with the string.

He hands them to us
and they droop a little,
bent like Fred's back
at the end of long planting,
but I know they'll straighten
with water and sun,
pay Fred for the plants
and head for home.

Digging the holes,
then pouring in water,
clods of dirt like clumsy swimmers
fall in around the edges.
I take the plants
from the butternut's shade,
where a red squirrel believes
his statued pose has fooled me
into thinking he's a branch.

The scent of the leaves and stems
is on me, new growth in the air
as I mud them in, packing earth
around roots and leaving it loose
near the top to let them breathe.

Standing, I realize
this is the odor I've lived through
another winter just to smell again.

Then I step back, look at four rows
of tomato plants—another year
planted and growing in this soil
that is sacred as memory can make it.

SNOWING THE GO-BACK ROADS

Now that winter, she said,
There wasn't much snow
and so as the teams
could pull the sleds
loaded with logs
we'd snow the roads.

This one fella, though,
he didn't know much
about the Big Woods.
When they sent him out
to be the road monkey,
why, he snowed the go-back road!

She and her brother
sit at my table,
talking the woods into microphones,
the stories and songs
which grew out of camps
at the end of deer trails.
There cool water bubbled clear
and the men would eat a peck of potatoes,
a dozen pancakes and a pound of pork,
wash it down with a quart of coffee,
then tromp off into those big woods,
all cut down sixty years ago
but growing back now,
tall trees doubling my life.

My voice, which loses a little more
of that ease of inflection each year,
that slow thought into words which flow
like streams which carried log drives,
tries to find the way to respond
to stories of my little-known blood,
though when I listen back I know
what I'll hear myself doing—
snowing the go-back road.

THINGS YOU LEARN

Each place they are different
like the soil and the time of first frost.
Each place they are the same.

Move slowly,
turning soil with your hands,
each lesson an arrowhead
found in a furrow.

Around here,
old folks say,
plant your corn
until the 4th of July.
That's the last day for corn.

Put peas in
just as soon
as the soil can be worked
and there's still
chance of snow
melting into the rows—
white manure.

Pick the suckers
off early
when they sprout
from tomatoes and corn.

Practice slow
those things you learn.
Remember, you'll
never know it all.

Believe that, with patience,
you'll know enough.

RASPBERRY MOON

Picking,
birds singing all around me,
the first of the ripe
black raspberries,
blackcaps, we called them,
red-smeared face and hands
matching scratches on arms.
a small bear plowing
through field's edge tangles

and now picking them again
from those same bushes
planted by my grandmother
before I ever imagined breath,
canes which give more berries still
that all the hybrids
I've planted, mulched, manured.

Tasting these berries,
an old Iroquois song
comes into mind
and I realize
that in fifty years
some grandchild of mine
might be picking such memories.

Nothing fertilizes,
strengthens more
than long decades
of love for this Earth.

MEETINGS

Strange how the face
of a woman
in whom
you might have seen
no beauty short years ago
becomes transformed
because her eyes or
the curve of her throat
remind you of someone.

Perhaps this is
the way to grow old
more in love with this world
for each person we've known.

STONE MAPS

Pulling the first carrot of the summer,
a stone came up, caught in root hairs
the way a fist might clench a coin.

The oldest people who lived this hill
before my feet stood here traced
their lives in the shapes of stones.

Each rock held a pattern,
a map of this land
which, read right,
might lead them home.

I matched the stone's lines
to the shape of my palm,
seeking some chart beyond my eyes,
a road the wings of a red-tailed hawk
might trace across the sky.

Holding it, I began to feel
my heartbeat entering its rhythms, then
buried the stone again, uncertain
whether I was ready
for those directions it might take me.

MEMORIES OF MY GRANDFATHER SLEEPING

Blanket tight over his head,
knees drawn up to his chest,
my grandfather slept
in this room.

Each morning I would
pull back that blanket
the way one parts tall grass
to see if a meadowlark's eggs
have finally hatched.

I would wait one moment
before speaking his name
in a tone I recognized
years later in the voice
of a shaman shaking his bell
to call an ancestor's soul.

Slowly the old man
would turn towards me,
toward the eastern door
and the morning light
the way a planet turns its face
away from the stars and memories of night,
looking up to be certain
that it was me and not Death
calling his name.

What was it he held, while half awake,
in his circle of sleep
which I feel in mine?

A warmth which holds us
to the Earth, an umbilical cord
that neither life nor death
can ever break.

FOURTH HARVEST

I would have buried him
in this soil
where he helped lift
fifty generations
of corn and beans
from seed to air.
Instead he rests, as the County preferred,
on the hill three miles to the north
towards the mountains.

Each year the crops I plant
grow better and this August
I watch my son who knew him
for one long year
move with the Old Man's
slouch among the corn,
his long hair golden
as that of Mondawmin, Corn Spirit.
How, at the age of 6, could he know
to move his hands and shrug his shoulders
as the Old Man did
and speak with such clear certainty
of the spirits he feels
pulse in a flower, an insect's wing?

Each year, on that hill
to the north of here,
the frost and rain
work the slow combination
that will let the soil
unlock his flesh,
that will let him come,
as the dark waters flow,
downhill to where
his spirit waits: home.

CLEANING THE CHIMNEY

The peak of the old roof
slants forty feet up,
there my grandfather walked,
even when he was 80.
I follow his footsteps
with a rope and a feedsack
holding bricks to drop in
and clean out the flue.

Placing my hands
on each side of the chimney
I remember again Jim Bradshaw,
Sigma Nu and the autumn of '62
when we did handstands
on the metal rail
above deep Cascadilla Gorge.
His legs were always
straighter than mine,
his back better arched—
like a question mark—
a diver held in stop action.

That year neither of us fell,
even though we looked down
as they said we should not,
the quicksilver thread
of stream far below,
lovely in those
sweet seconds of risk.

The creosote shines
like a grackle's wing.
Half-filling the chimney,
charcoal fists clench tight.
Hot air from the woodstove
lifts dust past my face.

In 1963 Jim Bradshaw
left school for Nam
in an officer's green.
His last moment of balance
was held over Phu Bai
before Charley's rockets
ripped through his copter.

Twenty years later,
there's strength in my arms
to do one more handstand

where no one would see
except birds and the trees,
for neighbors and drivers
keep eyes straight ahead.

Instead I just stand,
finish cleaning the chimney,
give one more moment
to memory and height,
then, holding that balance,
go back down the ladder.

NEAR THE MOUNTAINS

NEAR THE MOUNTAINS

Near the mountains
footsteps on the ground
sound hollow

as if to remind us
this earth is a drum.

We must watch our steps closely
to play the right tune.

THERE IS A STREAM

There is a stream which rises
halfway down the mountain
My father showed it to me
place he found in a dream,
the withered spirit of an old Indian
leading him like a wisp of fog
to its banks
I shall go to that last water
when I am old
and my blood runs
like the sad Hudson River
heavy with the waste
of civilization
I shall go there
and wade into those clear ripples
where the sandy bottom
is spread with stones
which look like the bones
of beautiful ancient animals
I shall spread my arms
in that sweet water
and go like a last wash of snow
down to the loon meadow
in the last days of April.

IN THE LAST DAYS

Cedars cling
roots dangling
like disconnected wires
dry in autumn wind
above layers of sea-bed sediment.
Edges sharper
than ancient ice
fall off below them.
Heavy with green
aquamarine berries
they have woven in
a century
holding decades against
freeze and thaw.
Here, near the water's
deepcut call,
on the side towards
the setting sun
they help me to hold
against the days to come

FLOW

for Lawrence Older

The pole-trails are gone, muskrats
dig tunnels in banks where booms were anchored.
A hundred miles south, a man growing old
tunes violins & from the feathery strands
of the bow and the trembling strings
a song is drawn.

And as those arms were smooth in the draw
of a crosscut saw, cutting down
through the grain of old pine,
they cut through the years, sorrows
and the ache in bones which tire
sooner and more each year.

The old songs grow new each evening,
leaves grow again from winter branches.
The music goes out like water from
lake Tear-of-the-Clouds down Feldspar Brook
into the Opalescent and the Hudson's flow.

Near the mountains
footsteps on the ground
sound hollow

as if to remind us
this earth is a drum.

We must watch our steps closely
to play the right tune.

VOICES

A train's whistle
so distant
you feel it
in your bones
before you know
you are hearing it.

Silhouette against
the silence of the night
like the shape of Cedar Mountain
against the stars.

Each season, each hour,
high in the Kaydeross Range
a stream is rising,
ringing a bell among
granite stones,
flowing towards this place.

ROOTS

An abandoned house
far in the woods
saplings grow out
of the caved-in cellar

In one corner
some quills & a chewed
canoe paddle show
where porcupines stayed
& there are signs
that wayworn deer
have wintered storms here

Ferns uncurl
from the foundation
delicate antennae
of enormous moths

A child's name scrawled
on the grey board
of a leaning wall

Put down your load
this is a good place
to start

HOMESTEAD

The walls of the old house
lean away like friends
getting ready to leave.

At the edge of the yard
twisted grass holds down
the gray board fence
that is trying to rise
& stand like a circle
of protecting arms.

Footprints lead
past crocus & dahlias,
corn stalks & rustling leaves.

They belong to no one,
bits & pieces of you
left in them, returning
to the land.

CLEANING THE SPRING

Numbed by the cold
hands falling back
into the old
unconciousness
of stone,
I keep working
scraping away
the leaves and silt
of a dozen seasons
until it opens.

Then I no longer
feel the pain,
the weight of winter
gone away, flowed clean
with the trickle
of fresh water.

PROPORTIONS

On top of mountains
only the rocks
can keep their size.

Whole forests
grow next to a rain water pool
that can be spanned
by a hiker's boot.

Adding an inch
each century
the cedars twist
into the peak.

On neighboring mountains,
bright heads of other climbers,
tiny birds' eggs
brief as drops of dew,
shine in the summer sun.

CAMPING ON THE MOUNTAIN TOP

Fog settles, at midnight,
on the peak.
You wake, knowing
what the cedars felt
when you cracked the centuries
of their dwarf branches
for your cooking fire.

You close your eyes,
but mist sifts in,
grey moisture beads
the roof of the tent.
You begin to recognize
the whisper of moss
scuffed by lug-soled feet.

You huddle back
into the sleeping bag,
praying for sun,
remembering stories
of weather that stays
this way for days.

Now, only the ice
formed in your veins
keeps you from making
a dash for the lowlands,
broken limbs a price
you'd pay to be back
where slow voices of stone
cannot find their way
into your dreams.

BIRCHES ABOVE CHAPEL POND

Scarred where steel
cut into streaked snow,
meaningless scrawls
of bark-deep love & passing names
crawl like ants
around wounded trunks,
slender as the necks of swans.

One summer day,
down from Giant Peak,
we swam in water
so warm & fresh,
it seemed no none could drown
& we dove like otters.

Then, eyes blurred or graced,
we looked up at trees
that seemed clean as linen.
No messages on them
but those of the years
holding the seasons
as a deep lake cradles
reflections of old High Peaks.

MINK BROOK FALLS

Above the falls a trail of hair
& one leg dragged like a stick
where a deer in the Starving Moon
was pulled down by coyotes
who howl from Big Pisgah
these spring nights.

The earth is dark,
moist with the roots
of Intermittent Ferns
near the stream.
Small Brook trout whip
out of the ripple and
dive under rocks.

There is a song
the falls have learned,
cold as spring water.
Remember it
with the wild dogs'
voices
from the Night Sun's sky,
tune your dreams to it:
flow, change, survive.

GLEN BROOK

Glen Brook has cut
sand & leaf mold away
to bare granite
washed and smooth
in the flowing lace
of rain-swelled waters.

Standing on
that winding spine
you can imagine
yourself as a stone
turning turning
with current & seasons

heading slow to the Hudson
two hundred yards downstream.

HAWKS ABOVE THE HUDSON IN MARCH

Ice down the river
flows with a heavy snow
seems standing still
until a stone divides it
in the river's center.

The only sound
in the sky is the wind
of the hawks' wings
lifting over granite
ridges, bare winter trees,
the eyelashes of dawn.

MINK

On the other side
of the pot-holed stream
mink makes its way
with smooth snake grace.
Small feet take it
from water to rock,
into brush then back again.
Sees us, smells us,
shows no fear.
Looks our way
with water-dark eyes
on the other side
of the flow where
rippled rock
& silver fish
face into the lace
of current foam.

Its coat is dark,
night without stars.
Its teeth
whiter than cloud,
breath hot, quick,
flicker of a small flame.
Yet it is not hurried
as it makes its way
up & down the stream
then gone into ferns.

It leaves us watching
a long time, wondering
at something
we might have been
four centuries
or an ocean ago
when humans and animals
lived within stories,
eyes aware of each other
calm on opposite banks of the stream.

THE RIVERS

Countless strands of thread gather
shimmering under the falling day star,
a magic.

Drop stone among stone
and pieces still can be named,
but rain or tears,
the flow of a stream,
a glass of water
fall into the river
and become themselves no longer.

Nothing else has such magic as this—
except that river
made of the breath
of animals, plants
and the moist Earth.

In it every place
is downstream,
all around you
is the sea.

MY ANCESTORS, THE STARS

Look into the sky
and we shall see the same
stars though for each of us
the heavens may seem different.

Hunter and Bear,
Swan and Weaver Maid,
Great River of Heaven
or Milky Way,
the stars reflect
our human dreams
yet remain the stars.

Distant, familiar
as those who've died,
each day they vanish,
each night return.

Slovak, Indian,
Immigrant, Canadian,
I embrace you,
my ancestors—
close to me
as sunset to dawn,
no further away
than the width
of a fallen leaf.

SKINNING OUT THE LAST DEER

A fat one
tallow caked round the ribs

after a few deft cuts
we pull

hide strips off
like tape

my uncle & my father
move about the deer
the last one shot this year
front leg dangles
where the .303
exploded bone

an old ritual
my father a man
good with rifle
and knife

and though entrails
pull out in strings
no omens are read from them

though my wrists ache
in the cold garage
this is a gift
of his autumn
sacrament
which we shall eat

FINDING THE SPRING

No more than two hundred yards from the camp
where water flows cool enough from the tap,
my father goes thrashing like a bear
through raspberry tangles, seeking the spring
which he remembers here.

This afternoon as we walked the road
he spoke of those old men he's known,
roots deep in these hills as trees
along the Cedar River Flow.

"You ought to talk with George Osgood,"
he said, "And Byron Andrus had some tales.
I remember the winter of '28 when we
took a twelve point buck up on top of Pisgah."

& now, for the last half hour or more,
I've followed, diving like a rabbit into swale,
through whipping hop hornbeam, scrabbling stones
for a spring he drank from thirty years gone.

I find a rusty coil of metal,
a joke to make us abandon his quest.
It spins his memory's compass instead.
"That'd be from the truck the old Caretaker had."

Then he vanishes, quick as a trout in the ripple,
lost in shoulder-high brush, his legs as young
as that half-century of following sign.
I trail, without complaint, behind
knowing he'll find his spring again,
if not for me, then for his grandchildren.

IN WILDERNESS

Last night the loon's cry
was thin as the edge
between mist and rain.

It wasn't full of the real world,
like the chickadee's flute note
or the throated chuck
of the anthracite grackle
in the birches where sand bank
breaks into beach
carrying small trees
down, a decades-swift
flow into current.

It might have been easy
to forget that call
if I were truly sure I heard it,
stirring past midnight in the thin tent,
cut by ghosts of dream.
It might have been only
the whine of a mosquito
slipped through netting,
the breath of one
of those sleepers with me.

Yet because there was
the chance of a loon,
it changed the night,
because it sounded twice
before I turned again to sleep,
because it was distant
as that place where river becomes lake,
because it was here—
far from lights, roads,
all the shaky foundations of certainty--
in wilderness.

CANTICLE

Let others speak
of harps and
heavenly choirs
I've made my decision
to remain here
with the Earth

if the old grey poet
felt he could turn and
live with the animals
why should I be too good
to stay and die with them

and the great road of the Milky Way,
that Sky Trail my Abenaki ancestors
strode to the last Happy Home
does not answer my dreams

I do not believe
we go up to the sky
unless it is
to fall again
with the rain